the madsunstar chronicles

Viral Mody

Copyright © 2019 by Viral Mody. 551231
Artwork by Stephen Fleming
Library of Congress Control Number: 2018914427

ISBN: Softcover   978-1-9845-7030-7
        Hardcover   978-1-9845-7029-1
        EBook   978-1-9845-7031-4

Print information available on the last page.

Rev. date: 12/27/2018

To order additional copies of this book, contact:
Xlibris
1-888-795-4274
www.Xlibris.com
Orders@Xlibris.com

"The key to immortality is first living a life worth remembering"
—*Brandon Lee*

"I think I am a natural-born leader. I know how to bow
down to authority, if its authority that I respect."

—*Tupac Shakur*

ONE

Introduction

You are about to enter a world of theory.

In my head apparently. I never nor do I have any proof of this delusional world to this day. I had a glimpse of this world for the first time when I was about twenty years old. And now, more than twenty years later, I am still learning many aspects of this world that I cannot even comprehend and understand fully. It began with a simple seedlike statement.

I was in a state of flux and paranoia about relationship issues, and I was taking a lot of drugs at the time. My girlfriend (Shanyn Helena Barbetti) at the time said simply, "Everybody likes your sunglasses."

As she emphasized *everybody* in the statement, I decided at that moment to figure out who "everybody" was. I would figure it out.

From that statement, I practically built an entire delusional world around my mind's eye that I concluded to be true. Call it paranoia. Call it bullshit. Call it lies. I don't give a fuck. That was the beginning.

Now, as I reach the end of this term of nonsense and delusionary chaos, I am hoping that if you are out there, caught in flux in this delusionary world, you might be able to use this guidebook in order to survive as I did, in Neverworld, somewhere inside the Andromeda Galaxy.

Welcome to the Madsunstar Chronicles . . .

Two

Prison Tools

In a paranoid, delusional world, the inmate must have tools of survival.

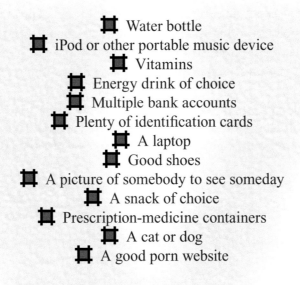

Water bottle
iPod or other portable music device
Vitamins
Energy drink of choice
Multiple bank accounts
Plenty of identification cards
A laptop
Good shoes
A picture of somebody to see someday
A snack of choice
Prescription-medicine containers
A cat or dog
A good porn website

Now I am somewhere I am not supposed to be, / and I can see
things I know I really shouldn't see / And now I know why, now,
now, now I know why / Things aren't as pretty / On the inside.
—*Trent Reznor*

Three

Inmates

You are an inmate in a prison without bars.

Trust nobody. Learn this strange concept early upon awareness
of possible paranoid, delusional entrapment.

Nobody can be trusted—not friends, family, strangers, social workers,
psychologists, or even a wife, a husband, or kids.

Most of these people are under the false belief system that they are helping you by
hurting you to some degree. This is a popular misconception that allows for those
other thieves, vagabonds, and some other filthy vagrants of society to use these
tactics for their own personal gain and perverse justifications of ill will.

EVERYBODY IS OUT TO GET YOU IN THE END!

In the beginning, depending on if you were born into this world or if you
are reentry, it is determinant on at what age you can trust people and how
much, until at a certain time, nobody is to be trusted. NOBODY.

If you have a "familiar," you can trust them. You can also trust cats, dogs, etc., but not fish.

It's OK to eat fish, / 'cause they don't have any feelings.

—*Kurt Cobain*

4

Four

Identity Crisis

Who are you? Ever wondered?

I ponder this question constantly. I know who I am to some degree.

My name is Viral Mody, born April 17, 1975, in Kadlec Hospital, Richland, Washington.

But who am I?

For us to be here in Andromeda Galaxy, Neverworld, we are here via

birthright

(born into a paranoid, delusional reality)

or

reentry

(inmate/prisoner [started at some point in life because of a crime committed]).

I was born in a small town, / and I will die in small town.
—*John Cougar Mellencamp*

FIVE

Omnipresent Awareness

Three Levels of Awareness

Level 0
Me (volunteer) and many others (prisoners/inmates)

Tabula rasa, unaware of anything abnormal about our reality

These people have started here from birth and are unaware when their sentence is complete and do not have any knowledge they ever committed a crime.

Level 1
Some (prisoners/inmates)

These people are aware they are serving a sentence due to a crime committed. These people are stuck here until their sentence is completed or pardoned.

Level 3
Tourists (general population)

These people are visiting this delusionary world. They may come and go as they please and are composed of most people in the world. They live in a different timeline (i.e., date in the future).

Things you've done have set you back in time, / I think about the way
we lived our life / was it yours or mine? / Why can't you tell me?
—*Lajon Witherspoon*

Six

The Last American Slave

No explanation necessary. Only one of my kind. A relic.

Me (volunteer).

I've got the understanding of a 4-year-old / I've got the
piece of mind of a killer soul / I've got the rationale of a New
York cop / I've got the patience of a chopping block.

—*Richard Patrick*

SEVEN

Immortality

Immortality is not an aspect of life that I am getting used to. Neither should you. If I truly felt immortal, I would be trying to fly with simply my arms and legs cascading the horizon. I just assume that I am immortal, because it is the only thing that makes sense due to circumstance.

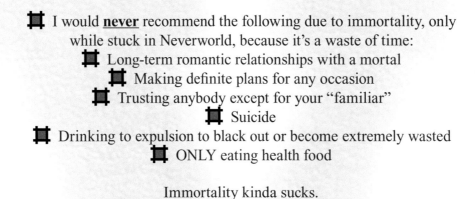

I would **never** recommend the following due to immortality, only
while stuck in Neverworld, because it's a waste of time:
Long-term romantic relationships with a mortal
Making definite plans for any occasion
Trusting anybody except for your "familiar"
Suicide
Drinking to expulsion to black out or become extremely wasted
ONLY eating health food

Immortality kinda sucks.

However, with some long-term goals, you can find the silver lining you seek amongst the clouds and you may fly through when the time comes that you may be an asset in terms of finding a new world beyond our own, a world that only an immortal could take the trip to.

Find your own long-term goals and stick to them.
My primary long-term goal is space travel.

It's all just a question of time.

—*Michelle Parylak*

EIGHT

Shit for Pavlov

The idea behind a Pavlovian dog would be a psychological concept that may
be loosely described as a system of rewards and punishments with an incentive
or the opposite in order to achieve a certain positive response.

When I take a shit, I am being rewarded. I am only able to shit when something of a
good or grand nature is occurring in the cosmos. When times are very good and I am
being a good doggie, I get to shit frequently. I am not sure if a dozen shits in a day is
abnormal, but I have been known to take that many shits in a certain given day.

As crude and strange as that sounds, you will notice if you have a mean streak
in you or are otherwise an asshole, you may shit very infrequently.

*(You might also notice a slight ringing in your left inner ear at a somewhat constant
basis during times of heavy constipation. I will explain your ears later.)*

Shitting has become a very pleasurable occurrence for me—and unbelievable even to
myself. I have come to long a shit almost as much as fucking a chick sometimes.

I have found some sort of temporary sanity in this;
/ shit, blood, and cum on my hands.
—*Maynard James Keenan*

NINE

Musical Broadcast

One of the only luxuries of being in a paranoid, delusional world is the theory that you may have a musical broadcast where invisible crowds would stop and listen to the music.

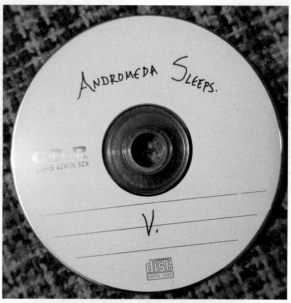

No explanation necessary.

You need a hobby.

—*Tara Ann Falvey*

TEN

Stigmatic Excuses

With regard to religious ideology, if trapped within a paranoid, delusional reality, it is best to keep your opinions inside regardless of your version of GOD or CREATOR or even if you are an atheist.

The tourists in this delusional world will use their perverse actions against you as just one more of the many reasons they feel justified of basically fucking you up.

Although very frequent in pop culture today, I personally believe a little in all faiths. I view religion mostly as folklore with different prophets arriving to our world throughout time. I find it difficult to find one religious perception as right in comparison to another regardless of age of conceptual idea. This is basically based on the premise of geological displacement that makes a Western religion different than an Eastern one, for example, based on where you were born. Although loosely stated, it is really what I believe, and the culmination of varying religious schools and scientific and spiritual thought led me to find one answer as cliché as it sounds: LOVE is my religion. Any religion that promotes love without hate is the one for me. But that's just me.

I have figured out most of this entire delusional world thus far through a linear path. Math and science. Having said that, some people—the dumb, the envious, the liars, the vultures, the thieves, etc.—will find ways to justify their own perverse actions of malignancy toward the blind (i.e., volunteers, prisoners, inmates) in this world by doing actions of malice toward us for their own personal gain. Nothing more.

This is wrong. There is no stigmata, release, or answer to be gained. Those concepts are propagated by the entertainment industry to give a partial justification as to why this delusionary, paranoid reality still exists. It is just one more reason to give them more money for their fat bellies.

Waiting, for your modern messiah / To take away all
the hatred / That darkens the light in your eye
—*David Draiman*

ELEVEN

The Smita and Vini Show

My parents are hosts of a game show called the *Smita and Vini Show*. I love my parents. They are the ones that raised me. From Nell Carter to Gary Coleman to Harvey Keitel and to all the Smitas and Vinays before and after that, who are alive or have passed, that's the bottom line. Although they are actors, we fight, we argue, we disagree sometimes, but they raised me. Well. And that's all the explanation you need about that. When you realize that your parents are not your biological parents, remember that they are the ones that raised you. And they are equally, if not more, important as a sperm and an egg.

I do not mean that in a mean way—it's just the truth.

Well parents are the same no matter time nor place / So to you all the kids
all across the land / Take it from me / Parents just don't understand."
—*Will Smith*

Twelve

Love and Trusting Only Yourself

(And Maybe Me)
In Neverworld, as I mentioned earlier, trust nobody. You will
not hear directly the excuses that range from

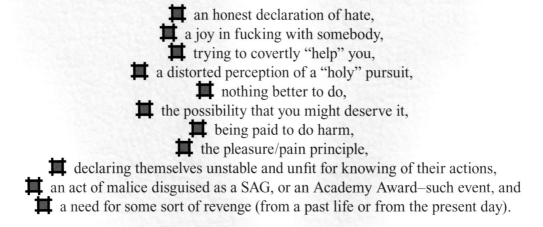

an honest declaration of hate,
a joy in fucking with somebody,
trying to covertly "help" you,
a distorted perception of a "holy" pursuit,
nothing better to do,
the possibility that you might deserve it,
being paid to do harm,
the pleasure/pain principle,
declaring themselves unstable and unfit for knowing of their actions,
an act of malice disguised as a SAG, or an Academy Award–such event, and
a need for some sort of revenge (from a past life or from the present day).

Remember the following mantra:

"I DO NOT CARE."

Don't worry, when you get through it, I will actually help you get the
revenge that they deserve. Trust me and yourself only.

Sing to me about the end of the world / End of these hammers
and needles for you / We'll cry tonight / And in the morning
we are new / Stand in the sun / We'll dry your eyes.
—*Lacey Sturm*

Thirteen

Kool-Aid Mentality

You will be called many evil things during your time in the paranoid, delusional reality. Andromeda Galaxy, Neverworld, is a breeding ground for vultures, sexually deviants, and thieves. They will justify their actions by discarding you with many words and names. Get used to words in earshot of your own self that might sound like

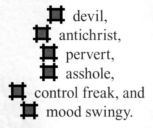 devil,
antichrist,
pervert,
asshole,
control freak, and
mood swingy.

But worst of all, your egotistical and grandiose notion that you stuck in a world of obvious observation will lead many people to simply depict and mention you as a wannabe cult leader of sorts. They will associate words such as *puppets*, *slaves*, and *brainwashed* to alleviate anybody who might want to be close to you as being simply dumb and mindless.

This not only leaves you isolated and in desperate need of human contact. The mere notion that you are trying to control others is somewhat funny because not only are people lying to you in its rampant form, but they are also controlling your mind as to what you know, see, touch, and feel.

They are the wannabe cult leaders, and they probably orgasm over the thoughts of bathing naked in a pool of Kool-Aid with you and some goats.

I don't know you, so don't freak on me / I can't control
you, you're not my destiny / Straight out of line / I can't
find a reason, why I should justify my ways.
—*Sully Erna*

FOURTEEN

Invisible Friends

Invisible friends might just be the only lifeline you have to some sort of normalcy and kinship most of the time. If the invisible friend is of the sex that you so desire—dependent on your gender preference, in terms of male or female— then you are in a good situation during the period of invisible friendship.

These precious illusions in my head / Did not let me down when I was defenseless / And parting with them is like parting with invisible best friends
—*Alanis Morissette*

FIFTEEN

Lifeguard for Frogs

Sports and athletics will be taught to you at an early age in many different forms. You will be gauged as to what you are good at playing. I played everything except hockey. I excelled only in swimming and skiing. Football, I sucked. Basketball, I learned to tackle people. Yes, basketball. Soccer, I sucked but was a decent goalie. Baseball, I was hit in the head by the pitcher on my first day out at bat during a real game and fell to the ground. Tennis, golf, and the . . . I could keep going, but regardless, I loved to ski and swim. I liked being around people, but within my own space, to move as a soloist. Having said that, along with a musical instrument and formal-schooling education, sports were heavily induced upon me as a young child while in Washington State.

I learned to swim and ski.

When you are asked what sports you enjoy, remember your childhood. All birthright delusional clusterfucks would have played sports, and some prisoners and inmates probably did by coincidence or design. But try and remember the intensity at which you played as a child—the fearlessness. Some people never lose that no matter how old and grey they get. Neither should you. You can apply it to everything you do, and someday, just as I did with my superior swimming capability, you'll rescue a frog while lifeguarding at Disney World. I told this story many times. The funniest part is that I was kidding. There was no frog, and it was never screaming for help. Ha. But if there was . . .

> I go out there and get my eyes gouged, my nose busted,
> my body slammed. I love the pain of the game.
> —*Dennis Rodman*

Sixteen

Failure Is Eminent

Prepare for failure. You might as well get used to this concept early. During your youth, you will be tested with very weird obstacles. They might not be very overt in nature during your early years. The obstacles will be easy to comprehend for you, although very confusing for the normal part of society. Once you have passed many ridiculous tests ranging from social, economic, ethical, and romantic situations, the real bullshit begins. Not only will you begin to be put into many easily ethical circumstances to learn toward bad doings, but you will also be set up sometimes and also coerced into doing things illegal to further prolong your stay in Neverworld. After some time, after mortals find your constitution too adept and strong to lean toward an overwhelming sense of uselessness, the severe manipulative tactics begin.

- You will make a joke about somebody or hurt somebody emotionally.
- Their relatives will swarm around your life like vultures under the guise of giving a shit about their relative that felt wronged by you.
- They will escalate things without regard for time and space. They do not actually care about anybody but themselves but will use their positioning to further motivate their previously criminal-intentive mind toward easy revenge tactics that will spiral out of control.
- They will continue to find justifications about the things they do to harm you and prevent you from finding indefinitely, until they are enduring consequences that brought them to your world in the first place.
- The cycle begins again. Vultures.

If you can endure the misgivings of these vultures and if you can persevere, don't worry. I will help you in the end. I have bargaining chips that are as unbelievable as they are true. In other words, we will bring them to justice. In the end. And I always complete something important to me. Throughout eternity.

I must be an acrobat, / To talk like this, / And act like that. / And you can dream, / So dream out loud, / And don't let the bastards grind you down.
—Bono

SEVENTEEN

Sexual Beings of Light

Sex is a big part of this delusionary world. Blowjobs especially. I am not kidding either. I do not know why the latter is so incredulously important; it just is. Most of you will lose your virginity about the age of seventeen to nineteen. It is irrelevant as to whether or not you are straight, gay, or bisexual. And do not let anybody tell you otherwise. Ever. Regardless of your sexual orientation, you will be made a mockery in terms of sex. Get used to it. In time, it will not bother you. It might be with regard to your pursuit of sex, your sexual orientation, or even the thoughts of sexual nature that you have, that again, are broadcasted unwillingly for the world to see and hear. It kinda sucks. But there is a silver lining. Before you reach the pinnacle in your life where the downward spiral begins, you will find sexual relations fast, easy, plentiful, and FREE. For the men reading this, get used to the idea of escorts and massage parlors. Immortality is good only in one MAJOR regard: we are STD-free. We are also capable of thinking a sexual experience to our partners during the act of sex or even from afar, such as while watching porn, which had been proven to be very gratifying to the partner that is the recipient. I recently learned this, and I wished I knew this when I had girlfriends during my youth. For the women reading this, get used to be labeled as a whore or slut very early in your twenties and beyond. You will always have a plethora of willing men to gratify you regardless of your appearance and constitution if you want them. I suggest that you pick and choose and find one person for a duration of time or simply embrace your sexual aggression.

Although it is very difficult to have long-term relationships with the same character role of somebody for a stretch of time, you will find comfort in the idea of that person. It is something to look forward to even if you never find that person again.

I am aware of how sexist it sounds that I wrote the differences between men and women and partners in such a manner; however, it is the truth, so that's enough.

SEVENTEEN (CONTINUED)

Sexual Beings of Light

By the way, I happen to be straight. This is irrelevant to anybody in Neverworld, but never let anybody tell you that you are wrong in how you feel. Trust yourself. Remember that. Trust how you feel, and as long as it is in the name of love and not hurt, you will be fine. Don't explain your sexuality. Just feel good. And although there might be a stint of time of loneliness and desperation, always continue to find romance—not just love, but romance too. A spark, a blowjob, or maybe even a simple kiss or hickey on the neck, a good sexual experience can bring you joy and sustainability in your delusional, paranoid reality for much longer than most mortals. You can find pleasure in a memory that most mortals have learned to overlook in life, it seems. Immortals have a sexual photographic memory that is more of a sensation than an image. For instance, I remember what one of my ex-girlfriend's neck tastes like when I would kiss and lick it. It's kinda weird, but that sensory experience has lingered in my head for a decade and, sometimes, makes me forget pain. Don't pay so much attention to what you see and hear but how you feel. Rely on the sexual nature of taste and scent. These types of senses are difficult to mask, and although they make you see and hear what they want, they cannot take away a memory of scent and taste. It's impossible.

By the way, use protection. A condom. I know I said that we are immortal, but if I am the only immortal, I do not want to be responsible for making a very serious error in judgment by telling you not to wrap it up or have it wrapped up. Ya dig?

Because there ain't no joy, / For an uptown boy, / Who just isn't
willing to try, / I'm so cold—Inside / Maybe just one more try.
—*George Michael*

EIGHTEEN

The Weather

DO NOT THINK ABOUT THE WEATHER. IF I TOLD
YOU, YOU WOULD THINK I AM CRAZY.

So crucify the ego before it's far too late / To leave behind this place so
negative and blind and cynical / And you will come to find that we are all
one mind / Just let the light touch you and let the words spill thorough
/ Just let them pass right through, bringing out our hope and reason
—*Maynard James Keenan*

Nineteen

Funny Farms

Do not be alarmed.

There is a good likelihood that at some point, or points, in your delusionary world experience, you will either be on meds or hospitalized for psychiatric reasons.

I was institutionalized four times in my life. At these funny farms, the walls are white and sterile, and the residents are doped up for the most part. You might encounter strange beings in these places. Two people that stick out in my mind are a guy whom I shared a room with that was a chronic farter and a suicidal chick whom I would later go to an S&M club with called R.U.S.T. in New Brunswick, New Jersey, near Rutgers University.

Normally, these people in these places are lost and confused.
They are in need of some serious counseling. Wait.

Did I say *these people*?

I am sorry, you might find one or two people in the whole fucking loony bin who are not actors. Do not be fooled. They are in the institution for no other reason than to either help you or hurt you.

I never knew at the times I was in the first three institutions that they were acting. I thought they were just really fucked-up people. I had no idea that we immortals would be immersed with SAG and Academy Award–type people within the confines of a mental-health community.

To them, our illness is art. It's kinda weird, no?

But I did meet a hot chick there, and you could as well. So embrace this crazy place when you arrive, and if you have my book to read, try not to laugh at the rejects in disguise as cuckoos.

It's not their fault they accept something such as this delusionary world as normal.
They are just blinder than you and I; they just can't see a bit more in reality.

Nineteen (Continued)

Funny Farms

If you are young and you feel that you can overcome going into a mental institution
and that this will have no deterring effects on your future, then take the help. I
personally wish I never went because now I can never be a cop. Oh well. I guess there
are more bad guys out killing people, because trying to keep me oblivious to reality
is more important than saving a human life. Kudos to the FBI! Just kidding.

If you are admitted into the funny farms, keep in mind that although you will suffer some tarnished
social aspects and job-like problems in the future, you will have one good thing happen: you will
be in a system, a system that can sustain you through the perils of the delusionary world. When
you are mentally ill, as I am—and keep in mind that even though I comprehend what I do not
see, I am still totally fucked in the head because of this process and probably always will be . . .

Anyway, when you are mentally ill, you might be able to adhere to the delusional reality
quicker if you accept that you are going to go crazy. I wish I knew that. I had no mental
guide. Nobody ever confirmed anything that I thought. Ever. Not even once as a joke.

I have assumed all these things to be true in this delusional world, from a pattern of insanity,
by picking up clues for almost two decades of retrospective thought and beyond.

You are fortunate. You will have this book. And I will show you how to survive. You could throw
my book away right now as you sit in your funny farm, or you could think, *What if he is right about
half of what he thinks?* Half is more than enough to make me a credible source of paranoid thought.

And let's face it. If you are going crazy right now, I am writing the book literally on
crazy survivalism. There are many medications that will be experimented on you.

NINETEEN (COMPLETION)

Funny Farms

Remember, being that you are not viewed upon as human, they will test many mind-altering drugs on you to find out not what works but what will stabilize you to keep you calm. They know that eventually you will figure some things out, and they really do not want you to die or commit suicide. I mean, if you did that, who would feed their fat bellies and propagate billions of dollars for various military and entertainment industries worldwide? Where would all the evil relatives of once-normal people flock to? What would they do?

Oh yes, keep in mind that they will keep you here until the cash cow dries, which is soon after you have read my book.

There are two kinds of people in life. Those who are out there to hurt you, and those who are out there to help you. The trick is to tell the difference between the two."
—*Erik Maldonado*

TWENTY

The Dope Show

Drugs are a big part of this delusionary world. This will occur at some early twenties or so point in your life. Give or take a year, you will find drugs easily and steadily at your disposal and decision. From marijuana for most and for others catapulting all the way up to heroin and crack, drugs will circumvent you. This is perpetuated upon you for three reasons:

▮ Entertainment. Viewership of your delusionary world. An interesting topic. Bullshit.
▮ To keep you here longer as their excuse.
▮ Your excuse for your insanity so other people do not feel bad or can blame their psychotic actions against you as more drug induced than their own perverted styles of fucking with you.

You will find yourself replacing blame toward others in time for your insanity and mind-altering chaos with ridiculous self-defeating statements such as the following:

"I wish I didn't do drugs."

"Maybe I tripped too hard."

"Drugs are too easy to find in the world."

"I shouldn't have taken drugs from that guy who offered."

Your self-guilt will be used as a tool for others to feed their own malice and vulture-like horns upon you. They will find every instance of drug-induced badness that you have ever done and use it against you forever.

With regard to myself, my drugs of choice were marijuana and LSD. Most of the time, I was stoned by myself and tripping by myself.

Am I still evil for smoking pot with my friends?

The Dope Show

As if I was an authority of some sorts. But if I was, you would not be reading this nonsense right now. My advice to you is simple. It is not a moral or ethical thing with me, but if you are in a stage of life where paranoia is already even slightly seen, remember the following mantra:

"SAY NO TO DRUGS."

I know how cliché that sounds, the antidrug statement of the world, and for some people, maybe slight drug use is OK for them. But for you, young immortal, think twice. If you were dying of an incurable disease, I would actually tell you to get stoned twenty-four hours a day if it made you feel better, BUT YOU ARE NOT.

If you succumb to drug use, you will not only be stuck here longer, but there are those who will think that giving you narcotics, unknowingly, is somehow justifiable. If you even think you have the slightest possibility of being in a paranoid, delusional world like myself, I would run from drugs like the plague. They will kill your soul. Being that you are immortal, the likelihood of overdosing is NULL and VOID, but your spirit will wither, and spiraling out of control will be eminent and sudden. Nobody will think less of you if you stay strong and stay away from things that hurt your body and mind. Use common sense.

I used to love getting high. It was fun. But the long-term aftereffects from other people in the Andromeda Galaxy, Neverworld, made for very uncomfortable situations and people of shallow caliber enthralling their relatives of even more dismal mind-sets around me.

Twenty (Completion)

The Dope Show

Drugs are just one of many different subthemes of this delusion that will be used against you and make one more reason for people not to trust or give you credibility with anything. Trust me about the drugs. Drugs kill. And if they do not kill your body, then they will kill your eternal soul.

Food is my current drug of choice now.

There's lots of pretty, pretty Ones / Who want to get you high / But
all the pretty, pretty Ones / Will leave you low / And blow your mind
/ They'll blow your mind / We're all stars now in the dope show.
—*Marilyn Manson*

TWENTY-ONE

Find a Loved One

Finding love and romance is a very difficult task in this delusionary world once you become aware that you are a volunteer, prisoner, or inmate of this dark and dreary place.

Before you are aware of your situation in the delusionary world, you might find a few love interests. Cherish those memories with that or those loved ones, and even if you totally fuck up your relationship, harness the memories that make you happy. During the latter part of your delusionary experience, you will find that romance is a luxury that will no longer exist.

The loved ones might discard you, leave you, or hate you in time, but that is irrelevant to your own memory. Try not to wrong the loved ones during the time you spend with them, but even if you do something that creates for a bitter breakup between both of you, carry their image in your mind and their voice in your ear.

During the darkest and most dismal times, those memories will give you the fuel that you need to keep on trucking through the Neverworld, Andromeda Galaxy, of paranoid and delusional thought.

Love is a gamble, and it's a safer bet than solitude.

Good Luck.

—*Shanyn Helena Barbetti*

Twenty-Two

Boy Scouts and Brownies Brigade

At some point during childhood, you will be introduced to the wonderful world of the Boy Scouts of America or Girl Scouts of America. For anybody not in the USA, there are usually similar programs for kids that teach good naturalistic skills and basic survival methods of life. Embrace these clubs. They are usually good and wholesome to encounter. You will find many attributes of life that will become very valuable in the paranoid, delusional reality that you will revert back to in blissful memory of your days during scouts.

Being a scout, or a Brownie, has its benefits during childhood and beyond, especially in Neverworld. I will explain why.

During childhood, being that you are an immortal, you are treated almost as though you are an adult/kid. While you must obey rules and regulations, you are always put to the test of the furthest point your natural-born ability will allow doing so. If there is a horse, while everybody is trotting, you are galloping. If there is a mountain to climb, you will be in front and be the one of the first to reach the summit and peak. If there is a fire to be built, you will find the kindling and make a fire using almost "magical" means. Aside from the social benefits of being a scout, or a Brownie, there is a rigorous and almost-methodical training on teaching you how to survive if shit hits the fan in reality.

I got my fist, / I got my plan, / I got survivalism.

—*Trent Reznor*

TWENTY-THREE

Lies, Lies, Lies

Contrary to all popular belief, it is OK to lie. Why not? In the
Andromeda Galaxy, Neverworld, we live in a world of lies.

EVERYBODY is lying to you and me.

For example, nobody is who they say they are. Their name, history, and most of the aspects of
their lives are more of a storyline than the truth about the person. You will encounter bullshit
circumstance followed by crocodile tears. The actors, musicians, athletes, etc. all playing the
part of your "friend" are all part of the circle of lies that you will encounter during your stay
here in Neverworld. It will be difficult to decipher the truth about a person, or the core per se,
and their character role will lead you to sympathize and even do things that you never thought
that you would do for a person. Their patterns of lies make all the crap that comes out of their
mouth full of lies too. They are so used to lying about who they really are, an actor for example,
that when they speak of emotion and circumstantial evidence about themselves, it is, too, a lie.
The funny thing is that you and I will be labeled the liar by most, because as a normal human,
past, present, and future become blended by your awareness level of this delusionary world,
and fragmented memories become skewed and distorted with time. This becomes your legacy
as a liar. So give it to them. Lie to the vultures and vagabonds. Why not? Fight lies with lies.

Sometimes, I intentionally change a story to verify to myself once again that I really am
in this world. And when you tell a distorted story to somebody, it's amazing sometimes
how accurately and precisely the story will come back to you in its true format. It's
as if the person WATCHED A FUCKING VIDEO about that particular event, which
they did and then retorted it back to you. Remember that I HAVE NO REAL PROOF
AT ALL THAT THIS DELUSIONARY WORLD EXISTS, so I have to remind myself
in some weird ways to keep my sanity, as you will find yourself doing as well.

And you never bother to wonder why, things are going so
well / You wanna know why?? / 'Cause I'm A Liar."
—*Henry Rollins*

33

TWENTY-FOUR

Replay the Tape!

The obvious question, or one of them, with regard to various actors
portraying your friends and family as character roles, is . . . ?

How do they know all the memories and factoids of your pasts together?

How do they know it AS IF THEY HAD BEEN THERE?

How do they remember the actual weather and the leaves
blowing across the lawn during the conversation?

How do they remember the smell of your cologne and which brand it was?

The answer is simple.

*They watch a video of your past with another actor portraying
their character role with you alongside.*

With the cameras in your eyes and otherwise, they can go to a conference audio- video room at
mission control and watch any films pertaining to you and the person that they are playing the part of.

To make this concept easy to understand, it's like Michael Keaton, Christian Bale, and
Ben Affleck all playing Batman and viewing their previous films with the preceding actor
playing the character role of Batman as indicators of how they act, move, and speak.

Every single day / every word you say, / Every game you
play / every night you stay, / I'll be watching you.

—*Sting*

35

TWENTY-FIVE

Everybody

Who is everybody to a prisoner, inmate, or volunteer in the
ANDROMEDA GALAXY OF NEVERWORLD?

Everybody refers to literally everybody who tunes into your life on the television
and multimedia crap on the computers that pertains to you. To the average citizen of
the planet, you are kinda like a sports team or something to watch. Nothing more.
Entertainment. Not even a real person. Kinda like an overinflated Barbie or Ken
dolls, but not as good-looking, however, can walk, talk, and say weird things.

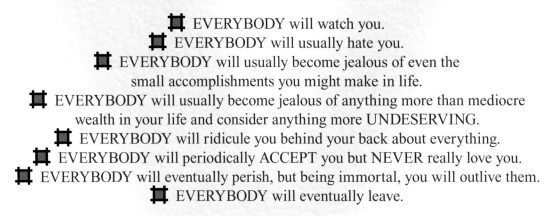

EVERYBODY will watch you.
EVERYBODY will usually hate you.
EVERYBODY will usually become jealous of even the
small accomplishments you might make in life.
EVERYBODY will usually become jealous of anything more than mediocre
wealth in your life and consider anything more UNDESERVING.
EVERYBODY will ridicule you behind your back about everything.
EVERYBODY will periodically ACCEPT you but NEVER really love you.
EVERYBODY will eventually perish, but being immortal, you will outlive them.
EVERYBODY will eventually leave.

Everybody knows it's coming apart / Take one last look at this
Sacred Heart / Before it blows / And everybody knows.
—*Leonard Cohen*

TWENTY-SIX

Shut the Fuck Up!

In the Andromeda Galaxy, Neverworld, there is a code, a code that *we* do not have to adhere to: SILENCE. Nobody is allowed to speak openly of this delusionary world. Like trained monkeys, our society has been taught not to ever utter a word about what is happening within the confines of this world. It is there, but it is in silence.

You will try to fight this code of silence and try to get answers. You will ask questions with no answers. Nobody will ever give you an affirmation, but they WILL give you a clue.

You will often hear the phrase "You're right" but not with regard to the delusionary world. It will be in another context, but you will learn to accept that the trained monkeys are just too weak and simple-minded to give you a direct answer about your confines. They have been trained well. And through experience and punishments for anybody who has broken this code, they simply shut the fuck up. It's kinda sad seeing people act so dumb. Don't try and rationalize the stupidity of it all. You will fail. Don't fight the SILENCE. You will fail and perhaps end up in the funny farm at some point sooner than you would normally get there.

Just understand that the modern society of man is in this way as primitive as the apes in the jungle.

Remember that nobody controls you or your viewpoint about this delusionary world. You can say what you want and do as you please to help others trapped here with us.

Fuck you, / I won't do what you tell me.
—*Zach de la Rocha*

TWENTY-SEVEN

The Thousand-Yard Stare

I stare. You stare.

When you look at things that are pretty to you, you stare and sometimes forget what you are looking at for a while, so much so that people begin to notice. This is one of the most frequent common denominators of those stuck in the Andromeda Galaxy, Neverworld. A fucking staring problem.

It's almost amusing, but the mental chaos that you will endure from virtually conception will cause you to stare intently at people and things. The drama that unfolds in your life makes a slight dent in the tabula rasa mind of yours, and without even being aware of such chaos, your eyes begin to fixate on things. Later in life, when you dabble in drugs and alcohol, you will find the stare more present, more evident. And people will make you notice that you are staring.

Most people don't like to be recorded unless they have vanity issues or are exhibitionists. Unless they are an actor, they do not handle being videotaped the same way as normal people. Your eyes are a video camera, and your eyes pick up any sound, which is then transmitted to mission control. This makes most normal people uncomfortable. Sometimes staring at people is almost fun.

In your eyes, the light the heat / In your eyes I am complete / In your
eyes I see the doorway / In your eyes to a thousand churches / In your
eyes the resolution / In your eyes of all the fruitless searches
—*Peter Gabriel*

TWENTY-EIGHT

Venom

The idea that you will be poisoned is a difficult aspect of the delusional-world reality to get used to. It's literally hard to swallow.

Frequently, you will feel "off." Your mind will tell you that you are not feeling well. You may develop a sore in your mouth or perhaps a pain in your abdomen.

Relax. It's simply people poisoning you.

This sounds very nonchalant. Mission control understands poisoning is a part of this delusion that they can't control when it occurs. However, they do know who does the poisoning and what methodology is used in even the most secretive and bizarre of circumstances. The people poisoning you will be punished; however, that doesn't really help the immediate pain you feel or the problems you might have with your body until the issue is resolved and they "repair you" in your sleep.

I still haven't gotten used to being poisoned countless times.

It's really fucking weird. I don't know how these people can actually think that they can get away with it in the big brother–type arena that we live in. The common idea of poison is somebody putting something in your drink. Well, sorry, but you will not only be orally poisoned, but the vultures will find unique and devious ways to poison as well by using everything under the sun—being cooked, being aloof, having panic attacks. Get used to it.

Being drugged is the easy part. But you must maintain your stability, because people forget that you were induced with poison when you act out from it, and they only seem to remember the action.

Always remember, "What comes around goes around." That cliché will get you by.

So why would you care, / To get out of this place, / You
and me and all our friends, / Such a happy human race /
Eat, drink and be merry, / For tomorrow we die.
—*Dave Matthew*

39

TWENTY-NINE

Cloak and Dagger

For reasons of survival, in the Andromeda Galaxy of Neverworld,
do not overthink the following concept:

Most everybody is in disguise, and they are doing so in order for your eminent destruction.
Your friends, family, acquaintances, and virtually everybody are wearing a cloak. They
pretend to love you. They pretend to adore you. They pretend to understand you.

However, it's just bullshit.

How is this possible? you might wonder. Being that we are actually somewhere in the future, i.e.,
past the second decade of the year 2000, many things such as this are possible. Your visual spectrum
deceives you. You are seeing what is imaged before you and not the reality of things. So you see
your brother or sister. Or was that really Gwyneth Paltrow, for example, in disguise as your sibling?

I should retract part of my earlier statement pertaining to everybody
cloaking themselves for your eminent destruction. There are a few friendlies
out there, in this sick world, but only a meager amount.

Anyway, most of the time, with regard to the character role that somebody is portraying, it is to
promote their movie of the weekend opening or perhaps an album that is coming out soon. They will
play the part for a little while and then vanish, allowing somebody else to play the part for a spell.

So nobody knows you. You are alone. No long-standing bonds or relationships. No constant memories
with the same person. When they say they remember an event from five years ago, they will always
remind you how that's not exactly how it happened and that they remember it another way.

Cloak and Dagger

Yeah, it's easier to watch a tape of a past event and make it a memory, as these vultures do, and ridicule you and call you an exaggerator or exacerbating events for not remembering every detail. So I learned a little trick a long time ago to keep myself in check when it comes to "remember whens." I mention this concept a lot. I frequently change it up, pertaining to an instance in the memory or event from the past, just to remind myself that I will be corrected, because the actor or actress pretending to be my friend will probably want to show off how they saw the actual footage of the memory and pimp it off as if it's their own and not another actor's.

It's confusing, this concept, I know.

But just remember these three points:

> ⊞ WE ARE NOT IN THE YEAR 2018 or 2020 or even close.
> ⊞ PEOPLE ARE IN DISGUISE ALL THE TIME.
> ⊞ MOST EVERYBODY JUST WANTS TO USE YOU somehow.

If you recall these three points and make it somewhat of a mantra, you probably will survive much easier here in the Andromeda Galaxy.

I'll give you everything you want / Except the thing that you want / You are the first one of your kind

—*Bono*

THIRTY

Mission Control

I theorize that in the beginning, mission control was the brainchild of a Stanley Kubrick–type director—a control freaky bunch of assholes, a group of people who directed others in this delusionary world. That was the beginning, as perpetuated by the notion that I am a volunteer.

As time went on and this delusionary world became more as a prison system without bars with inmates and prisoners and the hierarchy changed, mission control included not only directors and actors but also law enforcement to monitor those people who had been put into this delusionary world as a criminal.

Fighting mission control is useless.

I tried fighting for almost a decade after realizing I was in this delusionary world, full-blown in my early twenties. Now twenty years later from time of conception, I don't fight it anymore. I rarely even talk about it much. I am heavily medicated, and I just exist. I try and find streaks of happiness and bliss.

Mission control is not so bad. I think they believe that they are doing a service to humanity through the existence of this delusionary world. I have just witnessed too many flaws and inconsistencies within this delusionary world to be acceptable of it—this is from the perspective of a volunteer without any proof that this world even exists.

I will discuss the option of ending or perhaps bettering this delusionary world with mission control upon release from this unholy place of darkness. I do not know if they will listen to me, but I am leaning toward them having to. Why?

My latest theory is that I am part of the conglomeration of stupid actors and directors who created this place, to begin with, and mission control in the beginning. And I think I am right. But what do I know?

I am simply a paranoid schizophrenic with no proof whatsoever that I am living nothing more than reality, and this is the Madsunstar Chronicles.

CONCLUSION

There are a few aspects of this delusionary world that I intentionally did not address. I didn't mention certain actors' names that I believe are stuck here in this delusionary world. And I didn't address the beeps, blips, blops, and ear pain that I am subjected to for survival. If you read this memoir and are interested in knowing more, send me a message. Ask any question that you would like. I will answer honestly and openly. Remember, though, that this is all theory and everything I wrote has no proof or fact-based evidence whatsoever. This could all be bullshit.

Apparently, the delusionary world is all in my mind. And now the delusionary world is in your mind.

The mind is a beautiful thing to taste.

—*Viral Mody*

Printed in the United States
By Bookmasters